Confidence

MW00897317

Confidence Code And Hacks: A Girls Guide To Confidence, Self-Esteem, Self-Confidence, Skills, Charisma & Motivation

By Robin Forest

Thank you!

I wanted to start off by just saying thank you for choosing to read one of my books. I know there are millions of other books out there and how valuable your time is, so I am extremely grateful that you took the time out of your day to read my book.

Look at the end of the book to receive **FREE BOOK** from me personally. If you want to check it out right now, press >>HERE<<.

Table of Content

Introduction

Women usually feel pressure from society how they look and how should they feel in certain situations. This automatically affects our confidence and self-esteem. Research has shown that women are more likely to have lower self-confidence and esteem than men and more likely to spend money on their outfit and emotional well-being.

We are often worried about our look, the way we present ourselves and the impression we leave in the others. The truth is that a $500 dress but this will not necessarily increase your confidence, instead, you have to have the right mindset and follow certain actions.

Confidence is not only about self-fulfillment. Confident women are respected and admired, they often serve as a source of motivation to the others. Have you ever been impressed by the confidence of a woman? I am sure you did. Confident women face any fears that come on their way, they are usually risk takers and over achievers. They tend to find the positive side of their lives and respect themselves.

***

Before reading further, it is important that you understand what self-esteem and confidence are. On the one hand, having self-esteem simply means that you are happy with who you are, completely accept it and perceive yourself as "good enough". Thus, people who do not like you or do not accept your points of view are the ones who need to change. This assurance in your skills would impact the way you live and could stop you from reaching your full potential.

Confidence is about believing in your capabilities and not paying attention to other people's opinion. When you worry, it usually results in shying away from specific situations, individuals and is stopping your development.

Having healthy body and mind are essential confidence aspects and can help you in many other aspects. This is a very important area where exercise and diet have an essential role. Eating healthy helps keeping your body and mind in a good shape, which subsequently helps improving your self-esteem and outer appearance.

High self-confidence and esteem are qualities which are gained in time and people who want to improve them should put a lot of effort until they reach a satisfying level of both. It is not a team game and everyone is supposed to work on his/her own in order to develop them. If you believe that you are not competent, smart or attractive enough, this is just a state of mind and can be improved with a few simple steps.

One of the main reasons that restricts people from following their dreams is not being confident enough or being scared of failing... It takes quite some time and a good portion of courage to overcome this fear.

The good news is that you can.

"Low self-confidence isn't a life sentence. Self-confidence can be learned, practiced, and mastered--just like any other skill. Once you master it, everything in your life will change for the better." - Barrie Davenport

Everything leads to the important question: When you don't believe in yourself, do you think anyone else will?

Try the tips mentioned in this book. The most important thing is to read them and practice them every single day, starting from today. It is normal to fake it in the beginning and simply appear that you are confident. With time, you will find out that your self-confidence is growing rapidly. With practice (it is important to understand that this is not something that happens overnight), you will be able to become a self-confident, respected and admired woman.

Chapter 1: Avoid negativity and stay positive

Believe it or not, negative thoughts do not only have an impact on your confidence and self-esteem, but also on your overall life. However, this can be changed and now it is the time for you to realize that you should get rid of these negative thoughts. This is also the time to assess your close circle of friends, family and anyone you consider close. This could be difficult, but this is the perfect time to decide if you need to stay away from people who always shred your level of confidence.

A break from the Debbie downer in your life, even if it's temporary, can make a big difference and help you in focusing on becoming self-confident. Don't take this the wrong way, this doesn't mean you don't have to speak to your family or friends again, just try avoiding the ones that are always putting you down. This is the time to focus on yourself and improving yourself.

Be positive. Easier said than done and widely used phrase in the recent years, causing some suspicions how to be achieved. Being positive and enthusiastic when you interact with others, being excited to start a next project, no matter how small or big it is, meeting new people with open arms, everything helps raising your confidence level. Thoughts like: "I'm going to meet new people, will make a great impression and will definitely make new friends", should be a part of your everyday life.

Have an important meeting at work and full of doubts and fears? Replace this with: "I'm well prepared and will do an excellent job?".

Even though you might not be feeling it in the start, simply appearing positive will take you on the right track. Stop focusing on the issues you have. Something important you need to understand is that everyone has issues.

Do you think that your confident and positive colleague or friend doesn't have them? She probably does, the only difference is how she overcomes or perceives those issues. Start focusing on real solutions, dismiss negative thinking and start with small positive changes.

Negative thoughts have a big effect to how you perceive yourself, your life and even other people. Low confidence and self-esteem are often results of negative thoughts going in your head over and over again. If you believe that you are not good, smart, or attractive enough, this would lead to an endless viscous circle. You are what you believe. Always remember that.

"Be careful how you are talking to yourself because you are listening." - Lisa M. Hayes

This is what helped me run a very important marathon and train for it in only a year. I have always wanted to run a marathon but it was something that I found very difficult in the beginning. The truth is that it was not hard at all and everything was in my head. I replaced: "There is no way I can do this" with "I will train, work hard, and run the marathon successfully" and this is exactly what happened. I ran a marathon and finished it! It could sound vague, but trust me, it works. Learn how to eliminate those negative thoughts and you are on the right track.

Action:

Whenever you have negative thoughts, make sure you quickly replace them with positive ones. For example, instead of saying

"This is really difficult. I'm just going to do something else" (usually "something else" is sitting on the couch and watching TV, you know I am right), replace it with something positive like: "I can really do this, there is only a mile left for me to finish!". Whenever you have a negative thought in your head, you should replace it right away with a positive one, no matter how upset or unsure you are at that moment. With time, you will learn to do this automatically and you will improve your confidence and self-esteem.

Posture, eye contact, smile, the way you speak to the others are very important and have a big effect on your confidence and self-esteem. Standing up straight, something so simple, will tell others that your self-esteem is high and that you are confident. Smiling is also very important and often underestimated. Not only this will make you feel better, but it will also make people feel comfortable in your company. When you imagine someone who is confident, she most probably has good posture and often smiling. A small thing like this can cause a chain reaction, an investment which can pay off greatly. It also improves your energy instantly. When you wake up, go in front of your mirror and smile thirty seconds to yourself. If no one is around, try to laugh loud. It does wonders.

Positive body language and being happy is going to make you feel a lot better about your life and most importantly, yourself. Amy Cuddy, one of the leading world psychologists, found out that being happy decreases cortisol, the hormone regulating stress, boosts testosterone and confidence. Smiling, positive body language and standing straight is actually the easiest way to make yourself more confident and is definitely going to improve your self-esteem.

Therefore, this is just how important body language is and this is why you need to do your best to improve it as much as possible.

When I first started working in a multi-national company and my confidence was very low, my body language was clearly showing this off. Now, from the time distance, I realize that the way I placed my hands and the way I used to speak were sending wrong signals to the audience.

For instance, I used to speak to my manager and colleagues with my hands crossed. I was nervous and anxious. This reflected the image of myself as an insecure and defensive person.

How do you change that?

When you are speaking to someone, make sure you look at them directly in their eyes and maintain eye contact. Do not look at their shoes!

Speak slowly. Studies have shown that people who speak slowly feel and appear confident to the others. This would help people understand your point when stating it.

Action:

Dress appropriately, brush your hair and make sure you look great. You do not have to look like Beyoncé every time you leave the house, but you should at least look presentable.

Body language can be practiced. For example, if you usually do not smile, make it your mission and smile to everyone you speak to in a certain day. Smiling during simple interactions or even to the person working at the supermarket is more than enough and will definitely make you feel better. This is going to make you look great and feel confident.

Chapter 3: Empower yourself with information and knowledge.

We, women love talking (you know it's true) and there is nothing wrong with expressing yourself or admitting you do not know or understand something. Empowering yourself by knowledge and information, is an important technique for building confidence and self-esteem.

Have you ever had a conversation with someone and you were amazed how informative they are and wished to be just like them? The truth is that you can. Try to learn as much as possible about your job, presentation, or even something you find interesting. The good news is that the number of sources you can use is endless. The number of articles, e-books, and videos available online is enormous and you will definitely find a lot of sources you can gain information from.

Action:

Try learning one new thing every day. It can be about a topic you are passionate about, a random piece of info you found interesting, something related to your university, or even work. Do you find cooking interesting? Learn a new recipe every day and practice it? Want to improve the way you communicate with others? Learn a new technique every day and practice it with yourself and your social circle.

I remember once when I was having a conversation with a colleague at work and she clearly had no idea what she was talking about. She appeared not confident to me at all and there should be no reason why this could be you as well. When you know what you are talking about, this is automatically going to make you feel and look more confident.

Chapter 4: Be kind and have principles

The world would definitely be a better place if everyone was just a bit kinder. If you find this corny, then you are definitely doing something wrong and perhaps this is why your confidence might be a little bit low right now. Know that being generous and kind to other people and most importantly to yourself, is an excellent way to improve self-confidence because it automatically makes you feel better.

I have seen many people who are extremely kind to others but often neglect themselves. They even go an extra mile to help others, but when it comes to them, they forget all about it. This is completely wrong. You should behave to yourself the exactly same way you behave with the others. The key here is balancing.

Having principles in life is very important and has a big impact on your confidence and self-esteem. When you start helping others and treat them in a nice way, you will automatically feel times better. Treat people the way you want to be treated, the golden rule. When you implement the golden rule, you start feeling great about yourself. This is because you have helped others and you are one step closer towards being even a greater person.

What are the principles that you follow in your life? If you really do not have any or do not know what they are, then you are in trouble, because this means that your life might have momentarily lose its direction.

Don't you feel that it is important to treat people with kindness? Then this is probably why your self-esteem has not been that great lately. As mentioned above, the golden rule is the **key** to self-confidence and I try as much as possible to live my life based on it.

Think about the principles... Could it be that you have them, but you have not considered them that well or did not think about them that much.

Action

Try doing one kind thing every day. It can be to your colleagues at work, neighbors, friends, or family. Volunteering for a great cause or donating to some organization that you feel important, is a step to the right direction.

It can be something simple. Is your colleague having issues with a task at work? Why not helping out? Is your neighbor moving or redecorating? Why not offering some help? With time, you will notice that you are subconsciously helping other people and that this makes you feel a better person.

Always remember, you have to be kind to yourself first. If you are not kind to yourself, then you cannot be kind to others and being successful in doing so.

We are not perfect. I am not, you are not, and we probably never will be. There is a saying: "When in war, the wise learn to understand their enemy, really well". There is no way you can defeat an enemy without understanding who they really are. When you are trying to overcome negative thoughts with positive ones, the enemy is YOU.

You are the one who thinks you are not confident enough. You are the one with the negative thoughts in their head. You are the one who is not taking any actions to improve your self-esteem.

Let's change this.

Get to understand who you really are. Begin listening to the ideas in your head. You can even start a journal, write down the thoughts you have and begin analyzing why you have them.

I personally used to worry about meeting new people and was not confident enough to do so. When I started working on my confidence, I decided to go for it and learnt that this was all in my head. I went out, had a wonderful time and met great people at great places.

You should also write down the amazing things you know about yourself, what you are good at and what you love. Most of the time, you will find that the artificial limitations you have in your head are placed there by you and only you.

Writing down your positive sides, reading them loud or even sticking them on the wall, works as a positive affirmation and boosts your confidence.

Action

Start writing down weaknesses you have and work on improving them every day. Are you worried about meeting new people? Meet at least one new person every week. Worried about calling that guy you find cute? Try to speak with him. If he is interested, it would be great. If he is not, then it is his loss, not yours. Take it step by step until you accomplish your goals.

Chapter 6: Stop with the comparisons

We have all tried to be like someone else at some point in our lives. The important thing is to realize that you are unique. Their history is different, the way they are brought up is different and there is probably a lot that you are not aware of, when it comes to what they are portraying to the world.

The harsh truth is that there will always be someone who is better than you. The same way you are better than someone else in other aspects. There is no point in chasing perfection in every single thing. It is not going to happen. Ever.

There is nothing wrong with the wish to acquire a positive trait that someone has and this is where many people get confused.

Is someone you know really kind and always volunteering? This is an excellent trait and has nothing to do with comparing yourself. Do not forget that being kind is one of the best ways to acquire confidence as mentioned in the previous chapters.

If you want to copy someone, make sure you replicate the positive traits of this person.

Wasting energy and time trying to be someone else, fighting for someone's approval, is going to minimize your self-confidence even more and will not help you achieve your overall goals. When you are constantly comparing yourself, you are automatically placed in a failure line and guilt feelings will worsen your confidence.

Action

You can always start by writing down a weakness you have and work on improving it every day. Take it step by step until you accomplish your goal. Furthermore, if there is a positive trait that you would like to acquire, work on that every.

Chapter 7: Get out of your comfort zone

You need to work towards your confidence. As mentioned before, this is something that does not happen overnight. The reason I emphasize this is because many people think that this is something that will happen to them in a day or two. You cannot go to sleep not being confident and next day wake up and be a confidence queen.

If you do not speak during work meetings, then you have to start doing that. If you have three meetings during the week, try speaking up in one of them and see how it goes for you. The more you gain confidence, the more meetings you speak up in. As time goes, you will find that you are speaking up in every meeting that you have.

I used to be uncomfortable going and hanging out with my friends, if people I don't know are with them. I started to go out with them once per week, then two, then three times... suddenly I automatically gain confidence meeting people.

Getting out of your comfort zone is not only mental, but physical as well. You should do things that are challenging for you in a physical manner. This can include going jogging or even something more extreme like kayaking or kite boarding. When you are really focused on doing something challenging, you will be surprised how automatically your mind shifts. You become confident, comfortable and relaxed at what you are doing. You are definitely going to feel like a winner after a challenge like this. This is the exact mindset that is going to improve your self-esteem and self-confidence.

Yes, this is easier said than done, but the truth is the only way you can improve your confidence is by overcoming what makes you uncomfortable and is causing your fear. The key here is to do it the right way. Instead of saying just anything or shouting during the meeting, prepare what you are going to say and make sure you have notes with you. When you do this on a regular basis, your confidence is going to improve by time and you are going to get used to it.

Action

This week, try stepping out from your comfort zone a few times. For example, if you are shy and do not feel comfortable speaking to people at work, start by communicating to one person at a time every day at work. Once you are comfortable doing that, increase it to two people at work and so on. The more you do it, the quicker your behavior is going to become a regular habit.

Many women underestimate the importance of working out and eating healthy. Both of these have a positive impact and direct result on your confidence and self-esteem levels. Exercising and eating properly make you feel better both physically and mentally. When you look at yourself in the mirror and you are satisfied with yourself, this will lead to your higher self-esteem and confidence. Body confidence is an essential aspect of your overall confidence and one need to understand this.

I remember when I used to eat unhealthy food and was quite overweight. I used to consume mainly "wrong" food and never ever bothered to exercise. One of the main reasons why my confidence and self-esteem levels are high now is because I started eating properly, going to the gym three times per week, and improving myself both mentally and physically. I went from looking in the mirror every day and hating the way I look to looking in the mirror and being proud of what I achieved.

There are endless benefits from exercising and a proper diet. Exercising will boost energy levels and improve your mood. It helps releasing endorphins, chemicals produced in the brain to make you feel happy. 90% of serotonin is released from our gut. This is the chemical that is responsible for improving our mood. When you feel good, your confidence and esteem levels improve. When you don't, the opposite effect occurs.

You should always do your best to avoid taking antibiotics, junk food and food that is high in carbs and sugar. The Internet is your best friend if you do not have time to read cooking books, there are endless ideas available about how to eat healthy and tasty at the same time.

The main part of our confidence is a result of: the way we feel, how healthy we are and how we look. Confidence is a state of mind and body. Once you start eating right and working out, you will find a big improvement.

Action

If you do not have an exercise plan, make one this week. There is nothing called "I don't have time". I spend most of my time running back and forth to get tasks done and I still found time to exercise and cook healthy recipes.

Even the busiest people can exercise three to four times per week. It can be just half an hour every day. If you do not want to go to the gym every day, you should practice yoga at home. Instead of eating that unhealthy burger, try opting for fish with a salad. All of these are simple things that will not only improve your confidence and self-esteem, but also your health.

Conclusion

Confidence and self-esteem: two important qualities that many people aspire to have, yet find it difficult to achieve. Having the right level of confidence and self-esteem are two very important aspects that cannot be overlooked and might change your life. They are likely to change the way you perceive yourself and the way you perceive the people around you.

If you have problems in this area, you are not alone and you should take this as a temporary situation. Many women, including myself, have had problems with confidence. All the improvements I have gone through in these two areas did not just happen with a magic stick. To achieve high confidence and self-esteem level, you need to work on yourself, work hard and repeat.

As you see, building confidence in every aspect of our lives is extremely important. You can find it very hard to start, if you lack self-confidence, but once you start working on it, you see immediate changes. You can become one of those people, who are not struggling any more.

Being confident, usually means getting that project you were competing for in oppose to your opponent who is nervous, fumbling and overlay apologetic.

When you speak clearly, hold your head high, answer questions assuredly and when you honestly admit when you do not know something, it can just bring you that competitive edge you need.

Acting confident, you can inspire others to be the same. Imagine an enormous audience in front of you and you are killing it. Doesn't it feel great? Peers, bosses, your customers and their friends, all of them can eat out of a palm of your hand. The key way to find a success is to gain the confidence of others.

As you probably now already know, confidence is a skill, it can be taught and built on. It is well worth the effort. Work on your own confidence and build the confidence of the people around you.

Confidence consist of two things, self-efficacy and self-esteem.

Achieving the skill areas and goals that matter to you means that you gain a sense of self-efficacy. Meaning we learn that if we work hard, we will succeed. We accept difficult challenges, persist in the face of setbacks and lead the way.

Is it difficult? Yes. Can it be done? Definitely yes! You CAN become that confident woman that feels and looks great and is able to overcome all the issues that exist in her life. You can even inspire others and help them achieve that. Confidence is an excellent quality that we can transfer to our kids, families and spouses. The road to high confidence and self-esteem is not difficult at all. It might take time, but it is not difficult at all. Soon you will be able to become that confident person you have always wished to be.

The most important for you to understand is that this is all in your hands. You might read this book ten times, over and over again, but you are not going to see any improvements unless YOU really want to change. I spoke to a friend a couple of weeks ago who told me that she has not seen any improvements in her confidence and esteem levels even though she implemented some of the tips mentioned in this book. When I asked why she wants to achieve that? She said that it is because her boss at work commented on her confidence level. Her boss wanted her to change, but she did not, which is why there were no improvements. As long as you are doing this for all the right reasons, and most importantly for yourself, you will definitely achieve the desired improvements.

Take your time to read the tips in this book carefully and even go through them several times, if you need to. You do not have to necessarily do every single action and tip at the same time, but as long as you at least do something every day, even if it looks small, that is what matters. Make sure you implement at least one or two actions per day. With time, you will start doing these things automatically even without thinking on them. High confidence and self-esteem is something you can achieve. I did, others did, and you definitely can.

Believe in yourself and the rest will follow.

If you liked my book, please post a review. I value your feedback. You can post it at:

http://www.amazon.com/dp/B016VFTJSQ#customerReviews

Sincerely yours,

Robin Forest

FB Page: https://www.facebook.com/RobinForestWriter/

Get FREE sample of my newest book HERE.

My Blog: http://robinforestblog.wordpress.com, Twitter: https://twitter.com/RobinForestBook

I promise this is not my last book, so you are welcome to follow me on Facebook.

A Big Thank You!

I wanted to tell you first of all thank you for purchasing my book. This program has really made a big impact to my life.

Since the first time I made a decision to change my life, I've lost more than 22 lbs (10kg), my skin got clearer, my mobility is much better, I can do a split now, something I was never able to do in the past. But this are just the changes that other people can see as well.

The important change is within. I've became more confident, outgoing, made a lot of new friends, because I've changed the way I think. Being open minded, positive and conscious of my food intake has brought me to dimensions I never thought I can reach.

I believe you can do the same. I invite you on this exciting journey.

Kindness in words creates confidence. Kindness in thinking creates profoundness. Kindness in giving creates love. - Lao Tzu

Free Book

By purchasing this book, you get a FREE copy of my book Sugar Addiction. All you need to do is register at http://robinforest.me/ download the sample and let me know that you want the whole book. It will be send to you via e-mail.

Made in the USA
Middletown, DE
26 July 2017